MW00974675

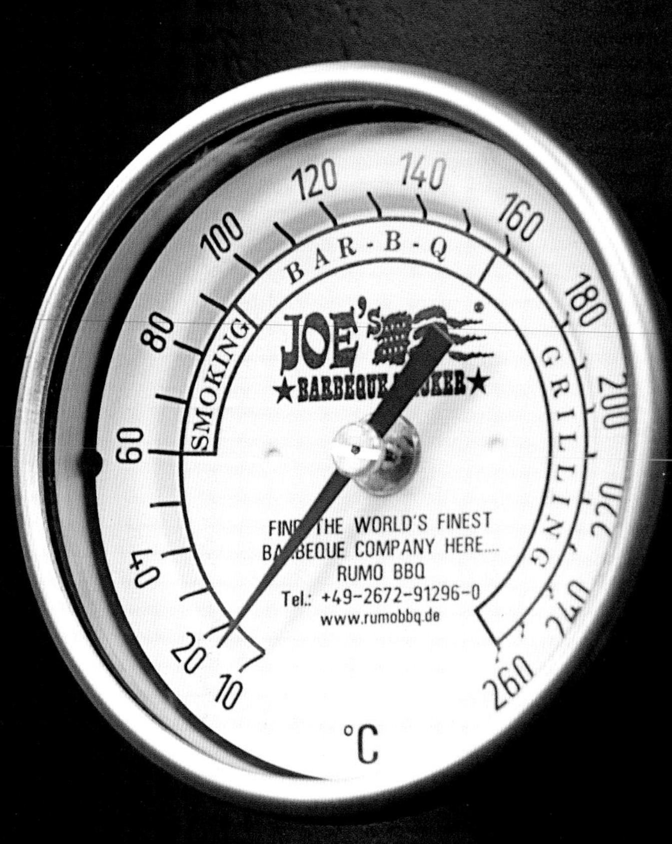
JOE's
BARBEQUE
SMOKING
BAR-B-Q
GRILLING
THE WORLD'S FINEST
COMPANY HERE....
RUMO BBQ
Tel.: +49-2672-91296-0
www.rumobbq.de
°C
10
20
40
60
80
100
120
140
160
180
200
220
240
260

OTHER SCHIFFER BOOKS ON RELATED SUBJECTS

THE BIG SMOKER BOOK
Techniques & Recipes
by Karsten "Ted" Aschenbrandt
ISBN 978-0-7643-4328-5

GRILLING LIKE A CHAMPION
Edited by Rudolf Jaeger
ISBN 978-0-7643-4498-5

COOKING WITH MUSTARD
Empowering Your Palate
by G. Poggenpohl
ISBN 978-0-7643-3643-0

Library of Congress Control Number: 2014955404

Originally published as *Das kleine Smoker Buch: Einstieg in die Königsklasse des Grillens* by Heel Verlag GmbH, Königswinter, Germany, © 2013 by Heel Verlag GmbH. Translated by Jonee Tiedemann.

Type set in The Sans & The Serif
ISBN: 978-0-7643-4772-6
Printed in China

Published by Schiffer Publishing, Ltd.
4880 Lower Valley Road
Atglen, PA 19310
Phone: (610) 593-1777; Fax: (610) 593-2002
E-mail: Info@schifferbooks.com

Project management: Christine Birnbaum
Layout and design: Muser Medien GmbH, Christine Mertens, Königswinter
Photos: Thomas Schultze page 1, 3, 4, 6, 8/9, 11, 12, 14/15, 17, 19, 26/27, 28/29, 30/31, 32/33, 35, 40/41, 42/43, 45, 48, 57, 61, 62, 67, 69, 70, 74, 80. Ramon Wink page 16, 18, 20/21, 22/23, 24/25, 36/37, 38/39, 46/47, 50/51, 52, 58/59, 60, 64, 73.

Franz-Christoph Heel, Editor

THE LITTLE SMOKER BOOK

GETTING INTO THE TOP LEVEL OF GRILLING

4880 Lower Valley Road • Atglen, PA 19310

Contents

A Few Words before We Start

This little book is intended for all those who are interested in grilling and smoking but who have not yet experienced working with a smoker on their own. Because these smokers represent quite a significant investment, you should be certain that your temperament and personality match that of a smoker. Smoking is not for people who are in a hurry and just want to pop up with a perfectly branded steak to impress the guests. And if you are eternally hungry, you will not be happy with a smoker ... that is, unless the smoker session is intended as a test for an upcoming week of fasting; six to seven hours with a permanent feeling of hunger while being outside is certainly a great test run for that!

If you want to be successful at smoking you need to take your time. A whole lot of time. Only then will you get the optimal results that make up for the many hours you spent managing the temperature and smoke dosage while waiting patiently. Guaranteed!

The basic techniques of smoking are explained here, including the most common types of smokers and tools, suggestions as to fuel, and several popular recipes. *The Little Smoker Book* is intended to provide all the necessary information so that you can find out whether this addition to the classic grill is worth the investment for you.

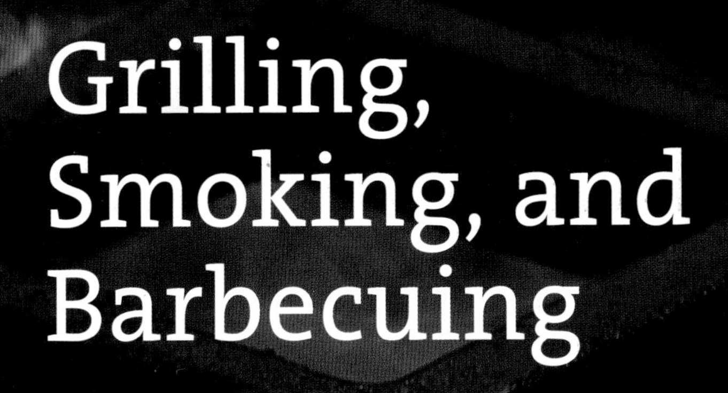

Grilling, Smoking, and Barbecuing

In order to understand the principle of smoking, let's review this method and its essential differences from grilling and barbecuing.

Grilling

The temperature should be high during the entire duration of the process. The goal is to achieve a nice brown and crisp sear. More tender meats, such as steaks or chops with little connective tissue, are best.

There is a distinction between direct grilling (temperatures between 320° and 570°F / 160° and 300° C) and indirect grilling (temperatures between 320° and 400° F / 160° and 200° C). When grilling directly, the meat is cooked right over the fire and flipped after half its total cooking time. Indirect grilling is not done over a fire, but over a drip bowl placed next to the fire. The meat is cooked by the smoke and the warm air, in other words, by the circulating heat. It works like a convection oven. Indirect grilling only works if you close the grill to provide the required air circulation.

Smoking

The original principle of smoking is to conserve the meat with a low temperature (under 100° F / 38° C) while adding a mix of salt and smoke. So smoking does not cook the meat. By reducing the water content of the meat the taste is intensified and the meat is conserved.

In earlier times the main purpose of smoking foods was to preserve them by using heat and smoke to remove moisture and to kill bacteria, but nowadays it is done mostly because of the taste: the smoked meat acquires a very unique note. The storability is a minor issue now, of course, in the days of modern conveniences.

-Q SAUCE
36 OZ. 1020g

Barbecuing

The two essential characteristics of a "real" barbecue are the low cooking temperature and the smoke, which is produced by adding either wood or charcoal. In order to barbecue the meat, the temperature has to be just above the core temperature of the cooked meat. For example, pork should be barbecued at 180° to 220° F (82° to 104° C) so as to have a core temperature of 160° F (71° C). Compared to the tender meats used for grilling, traditional barbecue meats have more connective tissue. Brisket has to be cooked slowly at low temperature in order to be able to eat it at all. Of course, you can barbecue all kinds of meats, not only the less tender cuts. It is suitable for vegetables, fish, and steaks. However, the main idea is to take advantage of the smoker's ability to add smoked aromas to food. So, for example, vegetables are not put into the smoker to be cooked, but to add a noble note of smoke to them.

The art of barbecuing consists mainly of reaching the required low cooking temperature and maintaining it, adjusting for possible changes in temperature. Temperature changes happen when opening the lid, or in the case of wind or rain or other adverse weather conditions, and they tend to prolong the cooking process. You will most likely need to practice under these conditions until you get the feeling for how much time you need to add under given conditions. There is really no way of predicting these changes in duration; the only method here is trial and error. If you want to have fun and success you not only need enough time to prepare the meats but also sufficient time to learn the "craft," to understand the smoker, and to adequately compensate for irregular conditions.

Barbecuing has a lot to do with feeling and instinct and experience. And certainly few if any pit masters can claim to know exactly how much charcoal or wood will be needed to reach the desired temperature so that the pork shoulder and neck are slowly conquered and turned into a delicious pulled pork.

You are definitely on your way to success if you manage to keep a constant temperature between 180° and 220° F (82° and 104° C). To control this temperature window, a thermometer is not only advisable but mandatory.

Difficult Choices — Which Smoker?

When you check out the range of available smokers, you will soon stumble over a few terms which you might not be familiar with. What exactly is an offset smoker or a barrel smoker? What is so special about water or bullet smokers and what distinguishes a ceramic smoker from the rest?

farmer grill

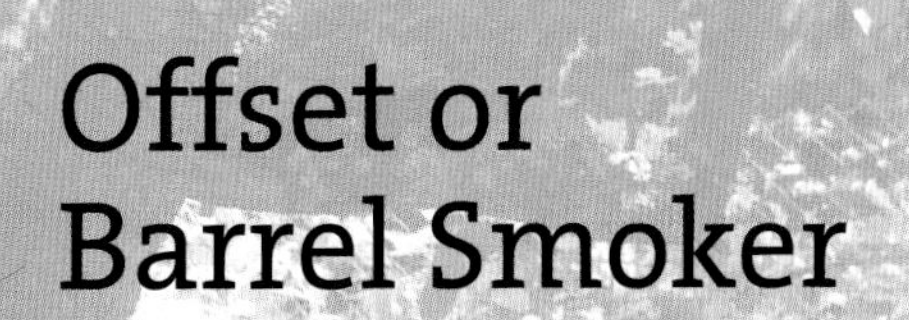

Offset or Barrel Smoker

For many barbecuers, this is the "genuine item" — you can barbecue with other models, but smoking with the offset or barrel smoker is certainly the most authentic method. The barrel smoker is a more developed version of the classic half barrel grill, which is made from oil barrels cut in half. The barrel smoker also has a support and wheels, so it's possible to prepare large volumes of meat that require extended cooking by indirect heat.

The fire in the side firebox, also called the burning chamber, produces heat that is circulated with the smoke around the food in the cooking chamber. The top of the side firebox regulates the intensity of the smoke taste. If you open it part of the smoke is released, changing the amount that's circulating through the cooking chamber. If you place a grill rack into the side firebox you can use it to do direct grilling. Be careful, though — you can burn things very quickly because having the grill next to the firebox makes it impossible to continue the cooking process indirectly.

When choosing a smoker, keep other features in mind besides the price and size; there are many details that will determine the quality of your life with a smoker. The manufacturing quality is important, the lid needs to be airtight, and its weight and the quality of its wheels both play roles. Keep in mind that as an ambitious grill amateur, you will most likely purchase a single smoker in your life, so this "smoker for life" is an investment you want to weigh carefully.

The following graphic describes how an offset smoker works.

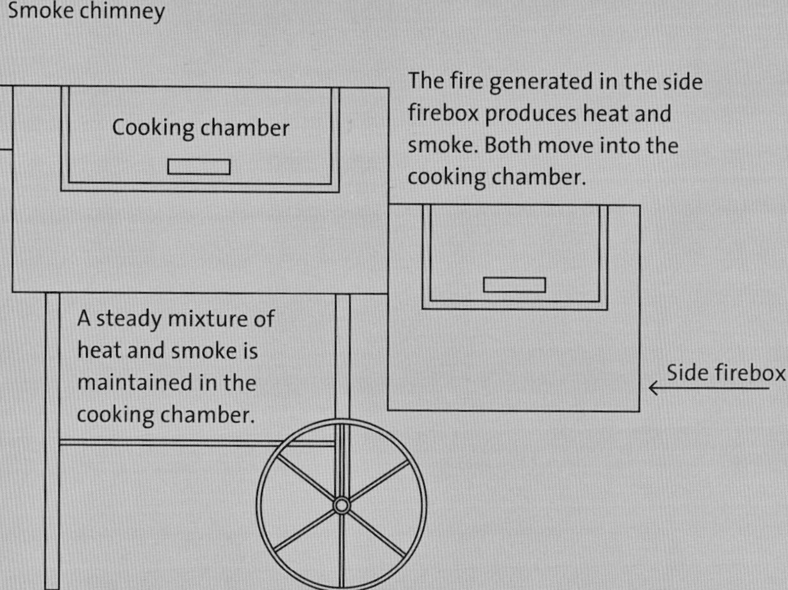

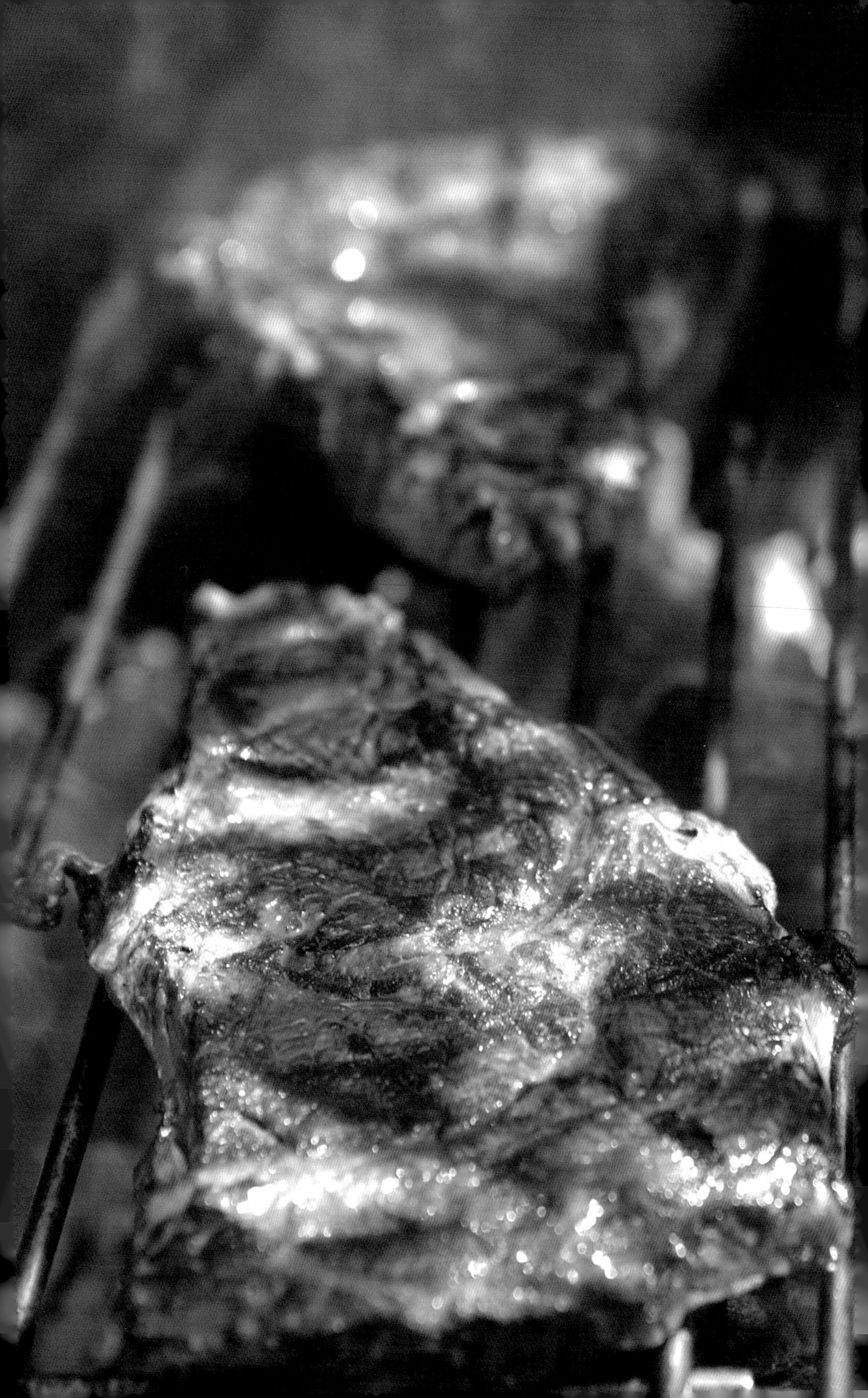

Water or Bullet Smoker

If you don't want to invest in an offset smoker and you don't have a large yard space, then a water or bullet smoker is a good alternative. Although it does not have the thick walls, it is easy to handle, which is a definite plus. Apart from the rather thin shell, the use of only one chamber is the other main characteristic. Where the offset smoker has different sections, the water smoker has it all under one roof: generating heat and regulating it, heat buffer, positioning of food items, as well as air intake and exhaust. The water is used to store the heat, and needs to be replenished continuously. If you want to avoid this you may place sand or stones into the bowl. This maintains the heat over many hours, and it is therefore well-suited for really long sessions; you can leave the smoker doing its thing, because a water smoker works for an entire day without adding fuel. An offset smoker needs regular provision of new fuel.

Ceramic Smoker

When you see the thick and usually green ceramic "eggs" for the first time, you wouldn't think they have anything to do with smokers. These ceramic ovens, which were invented 3,000 years ago in China, not only make for great grills or ovens, but they are fantastic for smoking, too. They need very little fuel and they keep the temperature steady over a long period of time — a primary requirement for successful smoking. Sliding doors allow for regulation of air intake and exhaust and a precise temperature setting.

And for all of you who want to try things out first to decide whether the smoked taste is attractive enough to you to justify the purchase of a "real" smoker, you can first upgrade a bowl or spherical grill with a so-called smokenator, a kind of smoker-light version. You can find out that way whether you were born to be a passionate smoker. It sure isn't your regular grilling anymore, but you might avoid making a bad investment — or, you may discover that you want more of it!

Big Green Egg

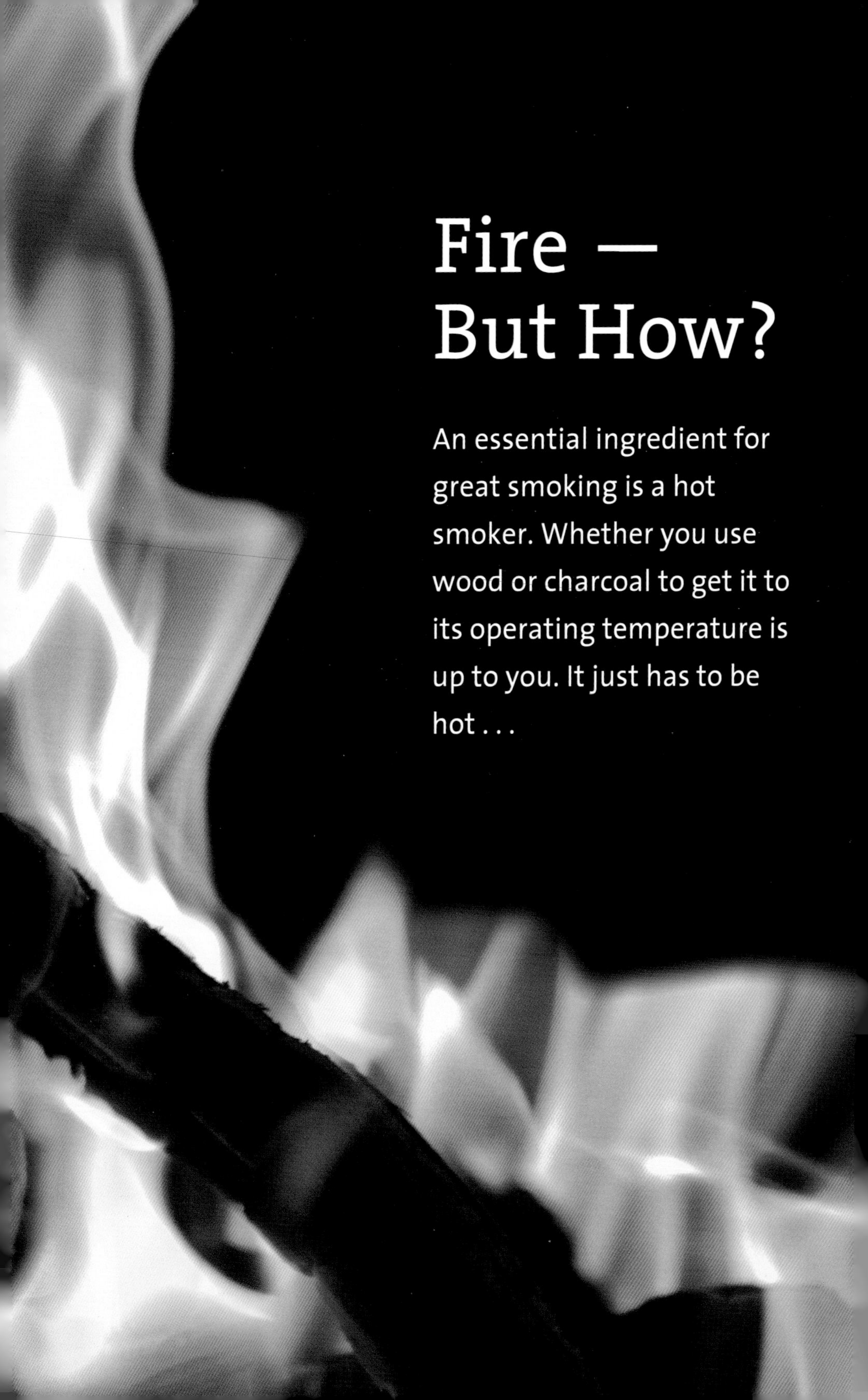

Fire — But How?

An essential ingredient for great smoking is a hot smoker. Whether you use wood or charcoal to get it to its operating temperature is up to you. It just has to be hot . . .

Firing with Wood

1) If you choose wood, you will need tinder (wood shavings dipped in wax work great) and dry, untreated wood. Place the tinder into the side firebox on the grill.

2) Pile thin sticks around the tinder in a loose layer, and place a second layer at right angles on the first one. The thinner the wood, the faster it will ignite.

3) Light the tinder in the center with a very long match or lighter. Careful; the flames grow quickly and can burn your fingers faster than you might expect.

4) After the initial burn has subsided, you have your bed of embers which provides the basic temperature. Place thicker firewood onto the embers. How much wood to add depends on the temperature you want to achieve in the pit. Close the lid of the side firebox.

Wood

For smoking sessions it is best to have several different sizes and thicknesses. When you start out, wood should be pretty thin with a small diameter (2 inches wide and about 10 inches long). To hold the temperature, it is ideal to have different diameters to react to necessary changes.

Next to the meat, the wood is the most important ingredient of smoking, so you should be careful when choosing it and keep in mind the kind of aroma you want to add to the meat. Different kinds of wood give off different smoke, so this is an important factor for the taste. For beef you can use almost any wood (apple, beech, mesquite, hickory, cherry, alder, or oak), while when smoking fish, you'd better skip apple, hickory, and cherry wood.

If you prefer a more mild aroma, for example for poultry, pork chops, or fish, then maple, fruit wood or beech are your best choices. Large pieces of meat such as pulled pork, brisket, or ribs are particularly tasty when you add oak, walnut, hickory or mesquite to the fire.

TIP

The smoke is regulated via the side firebox air intake. The less oxygen you let in (closed or almost closed ventilation intake) the more the wood smokes. Careful: without any fresh air the fire will extinguish and you run the risk of "oversmoking."

Charcoal or Briquettes

Firing with Charcoal or Briquettes

1) If you plan on using charcoal or briquettes with your smoker, you should place a rack into the side firebox to keep smaller pieces from falling through the openings. The rack also allows for ventilation from below and hence for a better overall burn.

2) Just as with a charcoal grill, it is best to use a chimney starter to fire up a smoker. Fill it with coals or briquettes, place the chimney starter on the rack, and light it.

3) First the coals or briquettes at the bottom of the chimney start to glow and smoke. Hot air rises up due to the chimney effect and ignites all of the coals or briquettes.

4) Once the coals or briquettes are covered with a layer of ash they can be spread out, since they are now fully incandescent.

5) When using charcoal or briquettes as opposed to wood, there is no smoke. However, it can be added by using wood chips as described in the next chapter.

. . . & Now for Some Aroma

If you are using wood to bring your smoker to operational temperatures, adding chips, chunks or pellets for additional smoke is simply an option. But if you are using briquettes or charcoal you have no choice but to use one of them.

Pellets

Pellets are mostly known as fuel for fires. But in the universe of the smoker, they play an entirely different role. They are used to create the essential smoke. However, they need a special treatment before they can provide their typical aroma to the food. Since they are fuel, they would burn right after being placed onto the briquettes or coals. And if you were to soak them they would fall apart. This is why pellets are placed into so-called smoke boxes, where they are protected from direct fire. These containers, made from stainless steel or cast iron, feature holes to release the smoke. Pellets are available in many varieties and mixtures, so you can find your favorite one.

BBQ DELIGHT
GRILLING PELLETS FOR SMOKE FLAVORING
MESQUITE
ALL NATURAL
100%
WOOD PELLETS
BBQ DELIGHT
GRILLING PELLETS FOR SMOKE FLAVORING
Sugar Maple
JACK DANIEL'S
Old No. 7 BRAND
Tennessee WHISKEY
NET WT. 1LB (0.45 kg)
ALL NATURAL
100%
WOOD PELLETS
BBQ DELIGHT
GRILLING PELLETS FOR SMOKE FLAVORING
HICKORY
NET WT. 1LB (0.45 kg)
ALL NATURAL
100%
WOOD PELLETS
BBQ DELIGHT
GRILLING PELLETS FOR SMOKE FLAVORING
Apple
BBQ DELIGHT
Smoke Stix
HICKORY
100% Compressed Hickory Wood
for Barbeque Smoke Flavor

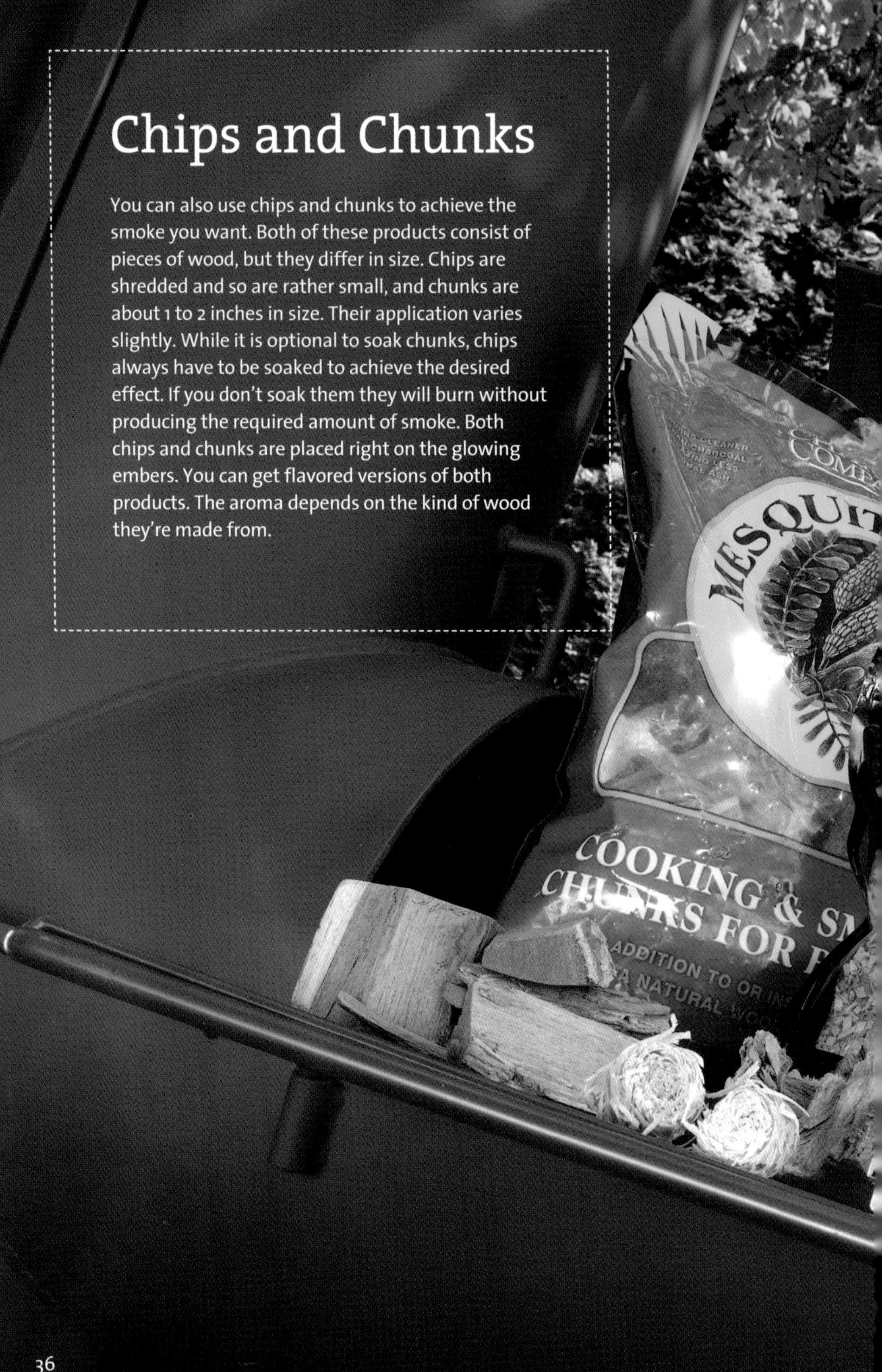

Chips and Chunks

You can also use chips and chunks to achieve the smoke you want. Both of these products consist of pieces of wood, but they differ in size. Chips are shredded and so are rather small, and chunks are about 1 to 2 inches in size. Their application varies slightly. While it is optional to soak chunks, chips always have to be soaked to achieve the desired effect. If you don't soak them they will burn without producing the required amount of smoke. Both chips and chunks are placed right on the glowing embers. You can get flavored versions of both products. The aroma depends on the kind of wood they're made from.

COMPANION
HICKORY
NATURAL AROMATIC HARDWOODS, SIZED AND DRIED WITH NO ADDITIVES
barbecook
barbecook
Oak flavoured

All Kinds of Gear

Some of the items are used for grilling, so you might have them already. But others are used only for smoking, like the mop. And heat-insulated gloves for pulling the pork are most likely not in the tool arsenal of regular grill users. (You should definitely get a pair of these, otherwise one of the most famous and tasty authentic smoker dishes, pulled pork, could turn into a painful chore.)

Brush, turner, tongs and scraper are items that ambitious pit bosses will likely not need to purchase, since they are already part of the universal tool kit. Several measuring cups and digital thermometers are often part of the grill gear. And certainly a good selection of quality knives contributes to successful smoking, no question about it. You might want to invest a little money here; it really pays off.

Checklist

A Feel for Slow

❐ Planning is everything. Smoking and spontaneity are incompatible. If you decide to smoke, you should think about what goes into the cooking chamber. There are several kinds of meat that need preparation before being smoked. Rubs and marinades are usually applied the day before the smoking so the meat can soak in the dry or wet mixtures. This is why it is a good idea to write down your plan a day or two before the smoking session. The smoker isn't really meant for spontaneous invitations. If you internalize the principle of "low and slow" beforehand you will enjoy the result.

❐ Do not confuse cooking times and preparation times. Particularly in case of the smoking classic, pulled pork, the difference between cooking time and preparation time is very significant. Once the meat is done, there is still quite a bit of time left before the grill master can serve the dish. The meat has to be further prepared and you need to add this time to the cooking time. So: read the recipes carefully!

❐ The meat needs to rest. Just as is the case with grilling, you should always keep in mind that meat needs its resting time. Your guests will definitely appreciate it.

A Feel for Hardware and Its Use

❑ Don't forget "burning in" the smoker. This is necessary to prepare the interior for the first smoking session and to increase the durability of the smoker. Burning in takes about two hours at 250° F (120° C). A thin layer of soot covers the steel and protects the interior walls when burning in.

❑ Keep the lid closed. The temperature is regulated via opening the firebox, never by opening the cooking chamber, which is only opened to mop, apply a sauce, etc., and which otherwise remains closed. Opening the cooking chamber increases the cooking time quite dramatically and the meat suffers when there are changes in temperature. There is a chance the meat may dry out or cook unevenly.

❑ Soak the wood chips. If you want to use wood chips for smoking then they need to be soaked before they can be used. This takes several hours, otherwise the chips will burn immediately and not provide any smoking effect.

❑ Check the wood. Use only dry wood and never any wood from conifers, nor any treated wood.

❑ Check the surroundings. The cooking times are just basic indications, you don't need to stick to them strictly. The real cooking time depends very much on the surrounding conditions. Wind, rain, snow — the temperature has a large impact on the cooking times stated in the recipes, so you will have to add time when conditions are adverse. Better to trust your meat thermometer, which shows you the core temperature. Be careful when punching in the thermometer and avoid hitting a bone, as that will result in wrong readings. You should also wait for some time before sticking in the thermometer to avoid juice getting lost early in the process.

❑ Of course the low-temperature cooking — low and slow — is all about smoke aromas. But be careful not to create too much smoke. The more smoke there is, the more the harsh smoke aroma will get into the meat. Less is more in this case.

❑ Remove ash. Remove all of the ash after each smoking session, as damp ash tends to corrode metal.

Timetable for the First Smoke

For the first ribs (recipe page 71) in the new smoker . . .

The Day Before

Get wood and/or charcoal; buy ribs, ingredients for the sauce, and the chosen side dishes

The Day of Smoking

09:00 AM

Burn in the smoker (about 2 hours). Keep in mind that this is a one-time procedure ...

10:00 AM

Prepare the sauce and place in the fridge to soak

10:30 AM

Prepare tools like cutting board, knife, marinade sauce, paper towels, etc.

Remove the ash left over from the burn in — this is also a one-time process

11:30 AM

Prepare the ribs for smoking, remove silver skin, place into pineapple juice for marinating

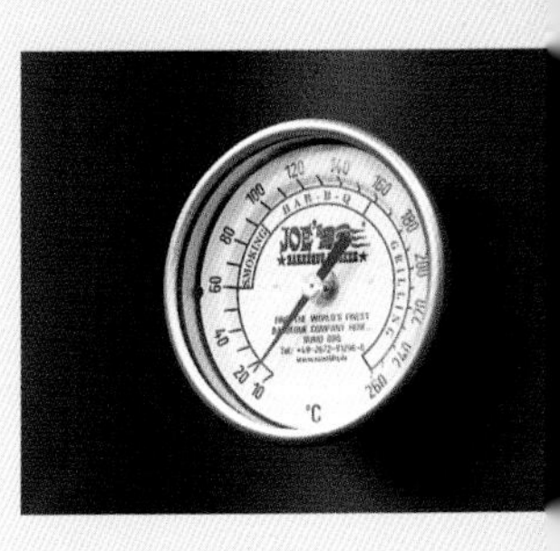

2:00 PM Chill beverages

3:00 PM Heat smoker to 230° F (110° C)

3:15 PM Remove ribs from the marinade, wipe with paper towel, add spices according to recipe...

3:30 PM ...and place into the smoker

3:00 PM During your first smoking session you should not leave your smoker unattended; watch it continuously so that you get a feel for the process and the changes of temperature that are possible. Make sure the temperature stays constant (use the slider). Regularly add wood or charcoal or a mix of both.

7:00 PM

4:00 PM Prepare side dishes such as salads and place in the fridge

6:00 PM Set the table

7:00 PM Take the sauce from the fridge so it reaches room temperature

7:30 PM Remove ribs from the smoker and place in aluminum foil and leave to rest for 5 to 10 minutes. Then slice into pieces and serve with the sauce.

The Day After

Clean smoker, and remove ash

Rubs &
Mops &
More . . .

Rubs and mops are inextricably connected to smoking. There are two kinds of rubs: the classic dry rub — that is, a mix of dry spices and herbs — and the wet rub. The latter comprises marinades and pastes. Both rubs are massaged into the meat prior to smoking. The meat is then sealed or wrapped tightly with foil so the spices are absorbed. Originally, rubs were used to conserve meat. Today, they are used to provide delicate aromas and to provide a delicious crust.

If you are using very lean meat, you might want to use wet rubs and pastes to avoid dryness.

To protect the meat against drying out while smoking, it is repeatedly brushed with mop sauce. It keeps the meat juicy and provides additional taste. The recipe will indicate how often you should mop the meat. In the case of long barbecues the mopping starts after about six hours. Lean meat in particular should be mopped repeatedly, because it tends to dry out quickly. Note that every time you open the lid to mop, the temperature in the cooking chamber declines, which prolongs the cooking time. The tools used to apply the mop sauce to the meat are actually similar to those used for cleaning purposes.

Rubs, Pastes, Marinades & Mops

for almost all occasions

Southern Succor Pork Rub

This rub is perfect for pork — from the shoulder to the filet.

Yields about 2 cups

½ cup freshly ground black pepper
½ cup paprika
½ cup Demerara sugar
¼ cup coarse sea salt
4 teaspoons mustard powder
2 teaspoons cayenne pepper

Mix the ingredients in a bowl. Store in a cool and dry place.

Basic Black Rub

It is almost presumptuous to call a mix of two basics a recipe. But this is an essential rub for the open-air cook. It is delicious for swordfish or tuna, scallops or hamburgers.

Yields about ½ cup

6 tablespoons freshly ground black pepper
3 tablespoons coarse sea salt

Mix the spices in a bowl. Store in an airtight container in a cool and dry place.

Poultry Perfect Rub

Chicken and other poultry works great with a large variety of rubs, so the choice of taste is up to you. If you ever try the following mix you will most certainly come back to it. Guaranteed.

Yields about 2 cups

¾ cup paprika
¼ cup freshly ground black pepper
¼ cup celery salt
¼ cup sugar
2 tablespoons onion powder
2 tablespoons mustard powder
2 teaspoons cayenne pepper
Peels of 3–4 lemons, finely chopped and dried

Mix the ingredients in a bowl. Store in an airtight container in a cool and dry place.

Wild Willy's Number One-derful Rub

A do-it-all rub, great for ribs, brisket, chicken and many others.

Yields about 2 cups

¾ cup paprika
¼ cup freshly ground black pepper
¼ cup coarse sea salt
¼ cup sugar
2 tablespoons chili powder
2 tablespoons garlic powder
2 tablespoons onion powder
2 teaspoons cayenne pepper

Mix the ingredients in a bowl. Store in an airtight container in a cool and dry place.

Primo Paste

This is a basic paste that is great for lean meat, particularly turkey.

Yields about 1 cup

1 peeled garlic head

6 tablespoons coarsely ground black pepper

6 tablespoons coarse sea salt

¼ teaspoon cayenne pepper or ground chipotle chilis

⅓ cup garlic oil

Grind the garlic in a mortar and thoroughly mix with pepper, salt, and cayenne or chipotle. You can also use a blender. Add oil until you get a thick paste. You can store this paste in a covered container in the fridge for about two weeks.

Kentucky Pride

This aromatic, smoky paste is great for fine pork and beef cuts.

Yields about 1¼ cups

1 medium sized onion, cubed

¼ cup bourbon

2 tablespoons brown sugar

2 tablespoons freshly ground black pepper

1 tablespoon vegetable oil

Mix the ingredients with an immersion blender until you get a thick puree. You can store it covered in the fridge for about two weeks.

Variation: **Texas Pride**

Replace the bourbon with beer or tequila. This version is great for chicken or wild fowl.

Roasted Garlic Mash

Particularly suitable for dishes with little cooking time, e.g., chicken breast or other poultry without bone, whitefish filets, small whole fish or beef filet. If you like, add a teaspoon of ground cumin, oregano or black pepper.

Yields about ½ cup

2 whole garlic heads

2 tablespoons coarse sea salt

2 teaspoons olive or other vegetable oil

Divide the garlic heads into individual cloves; do not peel. Roast them dry for about 6 to 8 minutes in a heavy pan at medium heat until they are soft and brown. Make sure the cloves are evenly roasted. Peel the cloves (easy after roasting) and place into a small bowl. Use a fork to mash them, and add salt and oil to achieve a coarse puree. Leave covered until you use it. The mixture can be kept for at least a week, although it gradually loses flavor.

Jalapeño-Lime Marinade

This temperamental mix sets shrimp and chicken on fire.

Yields about 1½ cups

1½ ounces pickled chopped jalapeños
¼ cup of the jalapeño juice
Juice of two limes
¼ cup corn oil
3 tablespoons chopped cilantro
4 finely chopped green onions
3 chopped garlic cloves

Use an immersion blender to get a fine puree. This is best prepared right before use.

Variation: **Lime-Jalapeño Marinade**

Switch the flavor and the name by replacing the lime juice with ¾ cup of limeade.

Mojo Marinade

Mojo is one of the great Latin American kitchen classics and is perfect for barbecue. The spicy citrus and herb brew is great for small pork filet chops, chicken breast or smoked onions. Keep some of it to use as sauce, too, because that's the original use of mojo.

Yields about 2½ cups

¾ cup fresh orange juice
2 tablespoons orange zest
¾ cup fresh lime juice
6–8 chopped garlic cloves
Chopped cilantro, to taste
¾ cup olive oil
2 teaspoons cumin
2 teaspoons dried oregano
1 teaspoon salt (or more)

Mix the ingredients in a bowl and use within a few hours.

Variation: **Spiked Mojo Marinade**

Spice up the marinade with ¼ cup of light or dark rum. Rum provides a slight caramelization effect on the surface of the meat and it helps the chef to "marinate" too.

Southern Sop

This is one of hundreds of the traditional pork mop variations that are common in the Southern states.

Yields about 3⅓ cups

2 cups cider vinegar

3 tablespoons freshly ground black pepper

2 tablespoons salt

1 tablespoon Worcestershire sauce

1 tablespoon paprika

1 tablespoon cayenne pepper

Mix the ingredients with 1 cup of water in a pot, and heat. Apply the sop while it's warm.

Bourbon Mop

This sweet mop sauce contains bourbon and is best suited for beef and pork.

1 cup Kentucky bourbon

½ cup brown sugar

½ cup finely chopped onions, almost blended

¼ cup sugar beet molasses (or substitute regular molasses)

¼ cup ketchup

2 tablespoons Dijon mustard

Mix ingredients thoroughly. You can store the mop in the fridge. Do not use at too high a temperature, since the sugar may burn. Thoroughly mop the meat with the sauce every two hours.

Rib Mop

This mop is perfect for pork ribs. The vinegar makes the meat tender while the herbs provide the taste. Apart from ribs, it's great for all kinds of pork dishes.

Yields about 1½ cups

½ cup water

½ cup vinegar

3 tablespoons mustard

3 tablespoons olive oil

1 tablespoon chili powder

1 tablespoon garlic powder

1 teaspoon cayenne pepper

Mix the ingredients thoroughly and keep the mop in the fridge. It can be refrigerated for about three months. Mop the ribs once an hour with the sauce.

Recipes

Pulled Pork, Brisket, Ribs, and Cobbler — these dishes are absolute classics and part of the art of smoking. But of course there are many more possibilities for enhancing food with a touch of smoke.

Pulled Pork

Yields 10–12 servings

2 pork necks or shoulders, about 5.5 lb each
2 tablespoons coarse salt
2 tablespoons ground black pepper
2 tablespoons paprika
1 tablespoon garlic powder
1 tablespoon cumin
1 tablespoon sugar
1 quart vinegar BBQ sauce (dilute it with vinegar if you like)

1. Mix the dry ingredients for the rub and keep them handy.

2. Dry the meat with paper towel, then apply the rub and the BBQ sauce. Wrap in plastic wrap and leave overnight to soak.

3. The next day, place the meat into the smoker and leave at 230° F (110° C) for 5 hours. Apply BBQ sauce every hour and bring to a core temperature of 195° F (90° C), which may take 16 to 18 hours. Do not raise the temperature of the smoker!

4. After cooking, wrap the meat in aluminum foil and keep inside a cooler box (without cooling sources!) and leave to rest for at least another hour.

5. Pull the meat apart, mix with some sauce, and serve in a bun with coleslaw.

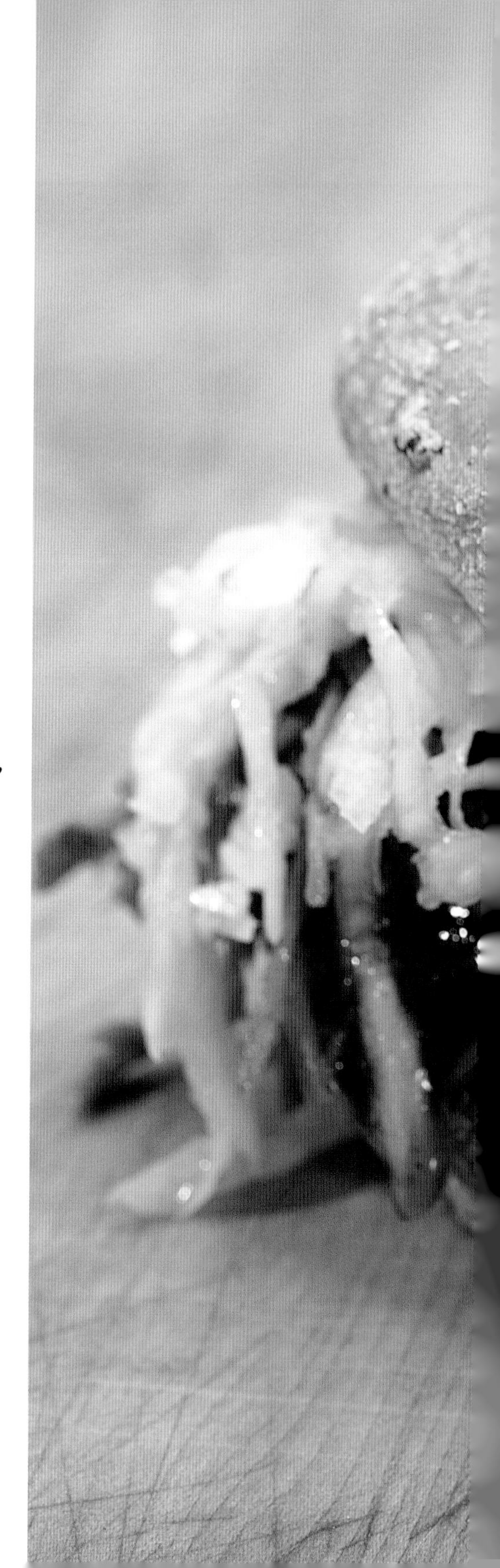

Classic Coleslaw

Yields 10–12 sandwich topping servings

6 cups finely sliced cabbage

8 green onions (including green parts) cut into thin rings

5 tablespoons sugar

1 teaspoon salt

½ teaspoon black pepper

4 tablespoons milk

½ cup mayonnaise

4 tablespoons buttermilk

2 teaspoons white wine vinegar

3 teaspoons lime or lemon juice

1. Mix cabbage and green onions.

2. Mix the other ingredients in a separate bowl, and season to taste with more salt and pepper if necessary.

3. Pour the dressing mixture over the onion and cabbage and stir. Refrigerate for about two hours.

4. Mix thoroughly before serving.

Non-Classic Brisket

You might cause consternation in Dallas with this recipe, but anywhere else it will be just fine to try it out. Against all tradition, this brisket goes into a brine, which turns the meat tender.

Yields 8–10 servings

Brine

½ cup salt
1½ quarts water
6 tablespoons sugar
¼ cup pickling spices

Non-Classic Rub

¼ cup freshly ground pepper
¼ cup ground coriander
¼ cup ground mustard seeds
6 tablespoons salt
2 tablespoons garlic powder

Meat

4½- to 6½-lb brisket

1. **Mix the brine ingredients the day before the barbecue, and place the meat into the mix. Refrigerate overnight.**
2. **Take the meat from the fridge four hours before the barbecue and wipe off the brine with paper towel. Allow the brisket to sit for two hours at room temperature.**
3. **Spread the rub on the meat and massage it thoroughly into it.**
4. **Heat the smoker to about 230° F (110° C) and smoke the brisket for 4 hours.**
5. **Wrap in aluminum foil and cook for another 2 hours.**
6. **Leave to rest in the foil for about 20 minutes after cooking, and then remove the fatty top section from the bottom section. The cut should be along the clearly visible separation between fat and meat.**
7. **Cut both sides against the grain and serve with a smoky BBQ sauce or with horseradish.**

Hot & Sweet Chicken Wings

Yields 8–10 main dish servings

4½ lbs chicken wings
2½ tablespoons freshly ground black pepper
1 tablespoon onion powder
1 tablespoon garlic powder
2 tablespoons chili powder
2 tablespoons chili flakes
1 tablespoon salt
Some oil
Sweet BBQ sauce as desired

1. **Place the chicken wings with all of the ingredients except for the BBQ sauce into a freezer bag the day before. Mix thoroughly and leave to soak overnight.**
2. **Heat the smoker to 250-265° F (120-130° C) and place the wings onto the grill in the pit. Close lid and smoke for 2 hours.**
3. **The wings are done when clear juice comes out after sticking a knife into the meat. Cover generously with BBQ sauce and smoke for another 20 to 30 minutes.**

Serve with additional BBQ sauce and provide sufficient napkins. If this recipe is too spicy for you, simply reduce the amount of chili.

Cowboy Beans

These beans are just perfect after a hard day on the prairie. Although the work space of many city cowboys is quite different these days, the taste of these Cowboy Beans has not changed at all.

Yields 8–10 servings

18 oz kidney beans (canned)
½ lb cubed smoked bacon
2 chopped onions
1 can peeled tomatoes, chunky
1 tablespoon chili powder
1 cup water
2 tablespoons Worcestershire sauce
2 tablespoons brown sugar
1 tablespoon mustard
1 teaspoon salt

1. **Render the bacon, and add all of the other ingredients except for the salt. Put the beans and the fat into a pot and place it on the side firebox or into the smoker at 230° F (110° C) and cook low with closed lid for 2 hours. Stir now and then.**
2. **Once the beans are tender there may be some liquid left over. Take off the lid and cook for another 20 minutes.**
3. **Taste; if the beans are not salty enough from the bacon, add some salt.**

Aloha State Ribs

Yields 4 slabs

4 slabs baby back ribs
2 cups + 2 quarts pineapple juice
2 cups crushed tomatoes
1 cup sugar
½ cup soy sauce
½ cup orange juice
2 tablespoons onion powder
1 tablespoon salt
1 tablespoon ground black pepper
2 tablespoons ground ginger
Pepper
Salt

1. **Boil all of the ingredients except for the ribs and the 2 quarts of pineapple juice in a pot and reduce until the sauce is slightly thick. Set aside.**
2. **Remove the silver skin from the ribs and marinate for 3 to 4 hours in the 2 quarts of pineapple juice.**
3. **Dry the ribs with paper towels and season with pepper, salt and ginger. Smoke for 4 hours at 230° F (110° C).**
4. **Cut into pieces and pour warm sauce over the ribs.**

Brined Dragon Drumsticks

Yields 8 turkey drumsticks

Brine

2 quarts water
1 cup salt
½ cup sugar
2 tablespoons onion powder
2 tablespoons chili powder
1 tablespoon garlic powder
1 tablespoon paprika
1 tablespoon freshly ground black pepper
1 teaspoon cumin

Rub

3 tablespoons onion powder
1 tablespoon garlic powder
2 tablespoons paprika
1 tablespoon freshly ground black pepper
1 teaspoon cumin
Some oil

1. **Mix all the ingredients for the brine in a pot, bring to a boil, and allow it to cool. Place the turkey drumsticks into the cold brine and refrigerate for about 6 hours. Then remove the drumsticks from the brine and dry them off with paper towel.**
2. **Thoroughly mix the ingredients for the rub and apply evenly to the turkey drumsticks.**
3. **Heat the smoker to 250° F (120° C) and place the drumsticks inside.**
4. **Smoke for 4 to 6 hours until the meat can be easily removed from the bone.**
5. **Place in aluminum foil and leave on a wooden board outside of the smoker for 10 minutes. Serve while still warm.**

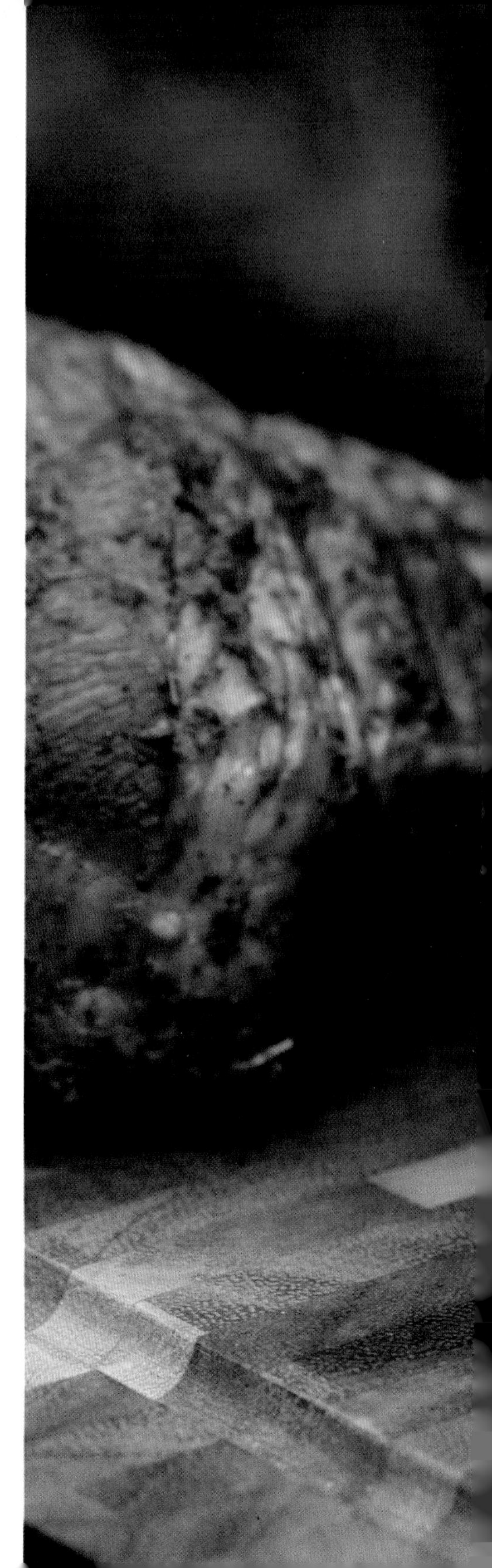

Homemade Smoky Almonds

2 cups shelled unsalted whole almonds
4 tablespoons butter
1 tablespoon herb salt
2 teaspoons sugar
½ teaspoon onion powder

1. **Melt the butter and stir in the almonds. Remove from heat and let cool for 10 minutes, stirring occasionally.**
2. **Put salt, sugar and onion powder in a mortar and grind to a fine powder. The finer the better!**
3. **Drain the almonds in a sieve, and toss with the spice powder to cover evenly.**
4. **Place into a shallow bowl and roast for about 30 minutes at 230° F (110° C) until they are brown.**

Store in an airtight container, or even better: eat right away.

Peach Cobbler

A cobbler is a kind of cake, usually with fruit, and there are two versions of it. In this version the fruit is placed into a thin batter that it sinks into. The dough rises with the heat and encloses the fruit.

Dough

2 cups flour
1 teaspoon baking powder
1 teaspoon salt
3 eggs
1 cup butter
½ cup crème frâiche
3–4 drops vanilla extract
½ teaspoon cinnamon

Topping

2 peaches, peeled and sliced
1 pinch nutmeg
Confectioner's sugar

1. **Put the embers in the side firebox to one side so there is space to bake, and heat the smoker to 350° F (180° C).**
2. **Grease a flat pan and sprinkle it with flour.**
3. **Thoroughly blend the dough ingredients and pour into the pan.**
4. **Arrange the peach slices on the dough and sprinkle with nutmeg.**
5. **Bake in the side firebox for 35 to 40 minutes. Garnish with confectioner's sugar before serving.**

Fruit Cobbler

For this type of cobbler, you first place the fruit into the pan and then cover it with the dough. You can use any seasonal fruit.

Dough

1 cup flour
½ cup sugar
1 teaspoon salt
2 teaspoons baking powder
1½ cups buttermilk
⅔ cup butter, melted

Topping

3 cups of seasonal fruit, peeled and sliced

Filling

½ cup water
4 tablespoons brown sugar
1 tablespoon cornstarch
1 tablespoon lemon juice

1. **Put the embers in the side firebox to one side so there is space to bake, and heat the smoker to 350° F (180° C).**
2. **Grease a flat pan. Place the fruit pieces into it.**
3. **Mix the ingredients for the filling. Bring the mixture to a boil, then pour over the fruit.**
4. **For the dough, first mix the dry ingredients, then add the butter and buttermilk. Spread the dough over the fruit.**
5. **Bake in the side firebox for 50 minutes. Serve warm.**

Barrel Smoker Maintenance

These sturdy barrel smokers are almost unbreakable, but after some time and exposure they tend to become unsightly, and that can be detrimental to the ambience of your yard! You only need a little maintenance and a few touches here and there to take care of this.

TIP You can use separating fat for cleaning purposes

Top: The passage of time — rusty spots form on the smoker, not a great sight

Center: After treatment with wire brush and sandpaper

Bottom: Spray with heat-resistant paint — it works like magic

After each smoking session you need to remove fat and ash and clean the grill. All you need is a spatula or scraper (for the fat), an ash shovel and a bucket (for the ash), and a wire brush (for the grill). If you perform this task regularly you are all set, as it will be easy to remove any leftovers and dirt.

First use the spatula or scraper to remove most of the fat, then apply hot water with dishwashing soap for fine tuning. It is best to use a garden hose to rinse the cooking chamber and side firebox after removing the ash. Leave the lid of the cooking chamber open so it can dry.

Because smokers are kept outside permanently, they tend to oxidize. Use a wire brush and sandpaper to get rid of the rust. First, brush the rusty sections to remove the loose rust. You can remove the resulting streaks and scratches with sandpaper, then wipe off the dust. Then apply a new layer of heat-resistant spray paint.